**Bypass Years of Struggle & Become Fluent in a Foreign Language**

# The Language Learner's Pocketbook

Cristian Dávila

**Product of Mezasu.com**

Copyright © 2018 Cristian Dávila

All rights reserved. This book or any portion thereof may not be reproduced or used in any manner whatsoever without the express written permission of the publisher except for the use of brief quotations in a book review.

Printed in the United States of America

ISBN: 978-1-7328376-1-4 (soft-cover)

ISBN: 978-1-7328376-0-7 (e-book)

First Printing, 2018

Unified Enlightenment

mezasu.com

Thanks to my Mom who spent countless hours correcting my many errors.

# **Table of Contents**

Foreword . . . . . . . . . . . . . . . . . . . . . . . xi

Set-up of the Book . . . . . . . . . . . . . . . . xv

Diving into Languages. . . . . . . . . . . . . . . . 1

  Introduction . . . . . . . . . . . . . . . . . . . . . . 3

  The Levels of Proficiency . . . . . . . . . . . 6

  Calculating the Time. . . . . . . . . . . . . . . 12

    Setting Your Goals. . . . . . . . . . . . . . . 14

    Set Your Goals . . . . . . . . . . . . . . . . . 16

    How Long to Learn a Language?. . . . . 17

    Your Hours to Reach Fluency . . . . . . . 22

    The End Goal . . . . . . . . . . . . . . . . . . 24

  The Romance Period . . . . . . . . . . . . . . 26

  The Four Phases of Learning. . . . . . . . . 29

    Comprehension. . . . . . . . . . . . . . . . . 29

    Understanding . . . . . . . . . . . . . . . . . 30

    Reproduction . . . . . . . . . . . . . . . . . . 31

- Focus Funnels .................... 33
- Wall Measuring ................... 36
- Habit for Language Learning ........ 38
- Language Learning Methods .......... 43
  - Preface of Language Learning Methods . 45
  - Spaced Repetition ................ 46
  - Mastering Vocabulary .............. 48
    - Connections .................... 48
    - Mnemonics ..................... 50
    - Memory Palaces ................. 51
    - Vocabulary in Context ............ 54
    - What You Know +1 ............... 55
    - Passive Learning ................ 56
  - Mastering Grammar ................ 58
    - Writing, Writing, and More Writing ... 59
    - Over-Learning ................... 62
  - Mastering Listening ............... 64
    - Over-Listening .................. 64

- What is Good Audio? . . . . . . . . . . . . . 66
- Mastering Pronunciation . . . . . . . . . . . 69
  - The Musician Method. . . . . . . . . . . . 70
- The Game Plan. . . . . . . . . . . . . . . . . 75
- Preface of the Game Plan . . . . . . . . . . 77
- Overview. . . . . . . . . . . . . . . . . . . . 78
- The Game Plan . . . . . . . . . . . . . . . . 79
  - Phonetics (& Writing System) . . . . . . . 79
  - Beginner Level Textbook . . . . . . . . . 82
  - Four More Textbooks . . . . . . . . . . . 83
  - Vocabulary in the Four Phases . . . . . 84
    - The Filing System . . . . . . . . . . . . 85
    - Comprehension . . . . . . . . . . . . . 87
    - Understanding . . . . . . . . . . . . . . 91
    - Reproduction . . . . . . . . . . . . . . 92
    - Automatic Reproduction . . . . . . . . 93
  - Listening & Advanced Study . . . . . . . 95
  - Speaking & Pronunciation . . . . . . . . 96

- Parting Information................105
  - Preface to Parting Information........107
  - Culture ........................109
  - Money Motivation.................110
  - Misconceptions ..................111
    - Only Children Can Learn Languages ..111
    - Dreaming in the language ........112
    - Thinking in the Language.........113
    - Native Speakers / Immersion .......114
    - Learn One to Learn Another........115
    - Two at the Same Time............117
    - Watching Videos to Learn.........118
    - Free to Learn ..................119
  - Tutors........................120
  - Burn Out......................121
- Conclusion......................125
  - What Now?....................127

# **Foreword**

My name is Cristian Dávila. I may not be the most experienced language learner in the world, but after failing for so many years (four to be exact) something clicked within me.

I don't even count the four years in school. I only count the four long years of self-learning. I know I'm not the only one who has or will suffer through this, so I wanted to lay out all the key details here.

I believe most people fail to learn a language not because they can't, but because they don't know how to.

I want to remove the years of suffering so we can all improve ourselves and become better connected with the world by learning languages.

There is much more information on language learning than I'm able to provide in this short book, but this will, at least, cut any excuses you've ever made.

If you learn more beyond this; all the better for you.

If you can still find an excuse, you should learn more about having a growth mindset. I won't go into detail here, but having the right mindset is everything! Not only in language learning, but in life.

The only one stopping you is yourself.

> If you believe you CAN'T learn languages, you are correct.
>
> If you believe you CAN learn languages, you are correct.

---

Aside from this book I have been building a language learning platform.

(The website is Mezasu.com)

I'll tell you more about the site when you finish this book.

For those who don't want to suffer through
years of not knowing what to do.

# **Set-up of the Book**

This book is split into four sections:

Section 1 – Diving into Languages:

> Describes general ideas about language learning and proficiency and will help calculate goals to set yourself up for success.

Section 2 – Language Learning Methods:

> Takes you through the methods you will use during your studies.

Section 3 – The Game Plan:

> Lays out a roadmap for starting a language and introduces new concepts and personal tips.

Section 4 – Parting Information:

> Useful information that didn't fit into the other sections and also clears up misconceptions.

# Diving into Languages

# **Introduction**

How many hours have you studied? How many words do you know? Do you have a solid understanding of grammar?

Did I hear an, "Huh," out there? Don't worry, I was the same way. If you're like me, you jumped in and hoped for the best with no thought of how to track your progress in a productive way.

If you don't know what you are aiming for, you will never reach it.

We must understand the basic levels of proficiency first to be able to set our goals.

This is the most important part and is a vital step that most people skip. This is why most people fail at language learning.

I will use the Common European Framework of Reference for Languages (CEFR) as the basis of my descriptions.

# The Language Learner's Pocketbook

You may have seen this used in other language learning sites to display your proficiency.

The Levels are as follows:

| A1 – Beginner | A2 – Elementary |
|---|---|
| B1 – Intermediate | B2 – Upper-Intermediate |
| C1 – Advanced | C2 – Proficient |

\* Notice \*

---

I will be putting my own spin on the CEFR descriptions and will give you estimates of the number of words you should know through each level. All names, numbers, and descriptions are my own; built around the CEFR levels to try and give an easy-to-understand description of what each level holds. The Word Count is my educated guess.

---

Before I describe the levels, I need to define Active vs Passive Vocabulary:

> Active Vocabulary - Words that are understood [with] the ability to use them in a real context.
>
> Passive Vocabulary - Words that are understood [without] the ability to use them in a real context. (Ex. Able to read a word, but not able to speak it in conversation).

In the chart, all word counts are defined as Active Vocabulary. (Ex. 250 words means 250 words of Active Vocabulary)

Now for the levels!

The Language Learner's Pocketbook

# **The Levels of Proficiency**

| A1 - The Party Trick ||
|---|---|
| Up to 250 words | Beginner |
| You are able to produce basic sentences and phrases that will only be useful during a party gag or the first small interaction in the language. (Ex. Able to say who you are, what you do, and what you enjoy doing in your free time). This is the quickest level to get through, but the most important. The whole language will be based on the concepts learned in this section. It cannot be skipped. ||
| At this stage, you may consider yourself, "The Newbie" ||

# Mezasu.com

| A2 - The Tourist ||
|---|---|
| 250-999 words | Upper-Beginner |

This is where you are able to get around in most touristy situations. You can introduce yourself and talk about your interests at a basic level. If traveling is a part of your immediate plans: asking for directions, making reservations, or ordering meals will be a part of your skill base, however, it isn't a requirement. (Ex. On the internet, travel skills aren't needed.) This phase will further solidify the basic skills from A1, while adding more general concepts. You will notice that natives will have to use basic and slow speech for you to understand (almost like baby talk).

At this stage, you may consider yourself,

"The Semi-Proficient Newbie"

# The Language Learner's Pocketbook

| B1 - The Conversationalist ||
|---|---|
| 1,000 to 4,999 words | Low-Intermediate to Intermediate |

| This is where it gets fun! You can "actually" speak in the language, no baby talk... though, native speakers will still have to drop their level to match yours. If they go off at their normal pace, you will find yourself at a loss even with the most basic phrases. You can, however, get by in the language. Depending on how well you can get around the parts you don't know, some may consider you fluent...you're not, but you can at least pretend you are and even pull it off in the right situations. |
|---|

| At this stage, you may consider yourself, "Conversationally Fluent" |
|---|

| B2 – The S.S. Friendship ||
|---|---|
| 5,000 to 9,999 words | Intermediate to Upper-Intermediate |

| |
|---|
| This is where friendships begin. The natives will no longer have to drop their level of speech to fit yours. This is your turn to match the natives' level. They can talk at their normal rate and you will understand what they mean. You will, also, have the ability to respond with some speed. Word searching will arise, but you will have a way to work around what you don't know. |
| At this stage, you may consider yourself, "Fluent" |

# The Language Learner's Pocketbook

| C1 - The Worker ||
|---|---|
| 10,000 to 19,999 words | Advanced |
| This is where you can start performing at a professional level. You can work at a company that operates in the language and make your way through most, if not all, situations that happen in daily life. There will still be unique situations where you won't need the skills to talk fluently about a topic. These require special study which may not be necessary. (Ex. occupations you don't work in or school subjects). ||
| At this stage, you are definitely, "Fluent" ||

\* Most native speakers have about a 10,000-word vocabulary by the time they are 8 years old.

| C2 - The Specialist ||
|---|---|
| 20,000+ words | Advanced |

These are the ones who strive for native-like fluency in a language. To get here, you would have most likely lived in a country with the language for many years without secluding yourself from normal 'native life' activity. (However, if "truly" "TRULY" dedicated, you can do this from the comfort of your own home with the power of the internet – though it would involve not having a life at all ;p)

At this stage, you are,

"Highly Proficient"

The Language Learner's Pocketbook

# **Calculating the Time**

Pick the level you wish to get to. You might want to stop at B2 which is fine. If you don't plan to work in the country, anything above that is icing on the cake.

For the sake of this book, I'm going to assume a starting point of the Absolute Beginner aiming for a baseline (minimum requirement) B2 level.

Some of you are going to hate me…I'm going to make you do a little math. Don't worry, it's not too much.

This is the most important part to setting our goals. "Realistic Goals", not ones pulled out of thin air like, "Learn 5 new words every day".

I'm going to prove to you why 5 words a day is a terrible goal to have, if you want to become fluent.

## Mezasu.com

| Time to Go From 0 to 5,000 Words [Viewed] ||
|---|---|
| Words/Day | Time it would take |
| 5 | 2.74 years |
| 10 | 1.37 years |
| 15 | 0.91 years |
| 20 | 0.68 years |
| 25 | 0.54 years |

The key point about this graph is [Viewed]:

- These numbers account for the first occurrence of the words and do not take into account the time to develop them into Active Vocabulary.

- 5,000 words is the minimum requirement to have real fluency in the language, but with only one occurrence, you won't get fluent.

Would you be okay with taking almost 3 years to come across the base vocabulary once?

If you are dabbling in the language, this may be fine for you.

If you are serious about language learning, I wouldn't recommend anything less than 10. And depending on your goals, even that might not be enough.

It's time for you to do some math!

## **Setting Your Goals**

While setting your goals, don't forget to account for days where you might forget or where you want to take a break.

I will be using a 5 : 1 ratio, or 80%, during my example calculations. (Meaning: For every five days, you can skip one and still maintain the goal | AKA – 4 days on; 1 day off).

You can set your own ratio; for example, the workweek, 7 : 2 or 71.5% (5 days on; 2 days off).

Pick what works best for you; however, I would never pick a 100% ratio. While this would be amazing to accomplish, it leaves you no room for error. You will resent any day you miss and you will struggle to make it back up.

Don't forget, you can always work past the goal. The ratio allows you to create a stockpile over time.

In my 5 : 1 ratio, if I study all five days including the break day, I can add that break day as a backup for the future.

You can even use this to plan for vacations.

*  Helpful tip  *

---

If you don't know how many words you know, assume 0 and start from there, even if you believe it's over 1,000. The chances are, if you haven't counted, you have gaps in the words you know. It is easier to start from the beginning and fill in the blanks as you come across them.

---

# The Language Learner's Pocketbook

| Set Your Goals | | |
|---|---|---|
| Total Goal Words Known | 5,000 | |
| Current Words Known | 0 | |
| Total Additions Needed | 5,000 | |
| Time You Wish to Complete | 1.5 years<br>547.5 days | |
| Active Days of Addition | 80% ratio<br>438 days | |
| Words Needed Per Day | 11.41<br>~12 words | |

The Math

---

Total Goal - Current = Total Additions

Duration (Days) * Ratio = Active Days

Additions / Active Days = Words per day

Words per day (Round Up)

# How Long to Learn a Language?

This is the most asked question in language learning, "How long does it take?"

Vocabulary by itself can take a long time, but there is much more to language learning than vocabulary.

This next section takes you through calculating the time it would take to learn the language. The actual time may vary, but we can set a goal and aim for it.

Let me ask you, "How long have you studied?" Unless you started today, you would say, "A few weeks" | "5 months" | "3 years".

This can give someone a quick representation of the time period, but it doesn't show the time invested.

Always count in, "Hours of Active Study".

# The Language Learner's Pocketbook

Two people could both invest 100 hours into studying. One may do it in one month and the other in one year.

How many [hours] have you studied?

---

The Foreign Service Institute created a timeline to estimate how many classroom hours it will take to learn various languages. This could be found under the name, "Language Learning Difficulty for English Speakers" or "FSI Timeline". I will refer to it as FSI Timeline or Timeline from now on.

* Warning *

---

The FSI Timeline is created using native English speakers as the base. Meaning, if you are a native speaker of another language, the following timeline will change. (Ex. Korean is noted as one of the most difficult languages for a native English speaker, but may be one of the easiest for a native Japanese speaker).

---

The timeline does state the number of weeks as well as the hours it would take. Don't worry about the weeks, but we will use the hours as the baseline goal. The actual time will vary depending on how well you study.

As quoted from their official site, "It is assumed that the student has above average aptitude for classroom learning of foreign languages."

Since I'm assuming most people reading this are self-learners, we can use this as a goal, but not hard fact.

# The Language Learner's Pocketbook

| Category I |
|---|
| Closely Related Languages |
| Afrikaans, Catalan, Danish, Dutch, French, Haitian Creole, Italian, Norwegian, Portuguese, Romanian, Spanish, Swahili, Swedish |
| 24-30 Weeks (600-750 Hours) |

| Category II |
|---|
| Similar Languages |
| German, Haitian Creole, Indonesian, Malay, Swahili |
| 36 weeks (900 hours) |

| Category III |
| --- |
| Significant Linguistic and/or Cultural Differences |
| Amharic, Bengali, Burmese, Croatian, Czech, Finnish, Greek, Hebrew, Hindi, Hungarian, Icelandic, Latvian, Lithuanian, Mongolian, Nepali, Pashto, Persian (Dari, Farsi, Tajik), Pilipino, Polish, Russian, Serbian, Slovak, Slovenian, Thai, Tamil, Turkish, Ukrainian, Urdu, Vietnamese |
| 44 Weeks (1,100 Hours) |

| Category IV |
| --- |
| Exceptionally Difficult |
| Arabic, Cantonese Chinese, Mandarin Chinese, Japanese, Korean |
| 88 Weeks (2,200 Hours) |

The Language Learner's Pocketbook

# **Your Hours to Reach Fluency**

If you're learning a language on the list, input the amount of hours for that category and calculate your daily estimate.

If the language is not on the list or you are not a native speaker of English, give yourself an estimate based on the difficulty you believe it to be. In this situation, I will always aim for more than you need.

* Important *

---

In the example, I used the least amount of time possible, 600 hours, for a reason. Even with the easiest to learn languages, you will still need at least 1 hour of active study per day to get to a reasonable level of fluency in 2 years' time. Anyone studying less than that is not going to have significant results and will get discouraged more easily, which could lead to quitting.

---

# Mezasu.com

| Set Your Goals | | |
|---|---|---|
| Total Goal Hours Studied | 600 | |
| Current Hours Studied | 0 | |
| Total Hours Needed | 600 | |
| Time You Wish to Complete | 2 years / 730 days | |
| Days of Active Study | 80% ratio 584 days | |
| Hours Needed Per Day | 1.03 hours | |

The Language Learner's Pocketbook

# **The End Goal**

Many people have no end goal. Some would say, "Language learning is a lifelong journey! You should never stop learning."

While these are nice sounding words, they have hidden poison within them.

Of course, you should always strive to learn more, but language learning is a long and tedious process. Without an end goal, it's easy to lose sight of why you started in the first place.

Here's how I define the end goal:

> The point in time where you no longer need active study and be happy with the results you have.

The key word is, "Active".

We still learn our native language every day, but we no longer need the active study. You can if you want to, but you don't have to.

Where do you want your end point to be?

## Mezasu.com

This could change over time, but having one in the first place allows you to see the light at the end of the tunnel.

If you can't see the light at the end, even a little bit, your first instinct might be to quit altogether.

The Language Learner's Pocketbook

# **The Romance Period**

There is a window of time where everything is new and interesting, known as the Romance Period. There will always come a time where that interest fades. AKA – The End of the Romance Period.

Once that time ends, you are left with only your motivation to keep you going. The work could seem hard. The progress could feel slow. This is where most people drop off from language learning.

In my experience, it takes no more than 3 months' time for it to go away. The actual time period may differ for you, but whether you're studying for 5 minutes a day or for hours, this Romance Period will always disappear.

With your interest at its peak, I want you to take advantage of this time period and get as far as you can in the language.

# Mezasu.com

Don't slow down! If anything, I want you to work past the goals you set for yourself.

In the following chart, I compare times of study (per day) and how they add up over three months.

| Time Studied Over 90 Days |||
|---|---|---|
| Time Per Day | Hours | % of Goal |
| 15 min | 18 hours | 3% |
| 30 min | 36 hours | 6% |
| 1 hour | 72 hours | 12% |
| 3 hours | 216 hours | 36% |

* The numbers given account for the 80% ratio with 600 hours of the goal study time.

---

At the end of this time, where would you rather be? The more the merrier, right?

You should squeeze out as much as possible during this time period. The excitement of the new and interesting will allow you to sustain longer periods of study without added strain.

# The Language Learner's Pocketbook

Just strive for more. This is also preparing us for when the Romance Period ends.

Once the excitement fades, it could be difficult to stay motivated. Imagine taking three months to complete 3% of your total goal. Not fun!

Even the suggested time, one hour, may leave you unsatisfied and make it feel like you haven't gained a significant skill in the language.

Remember the usual answer to, "How long have you studied?"

We will always think back to the weeks, months, and years spent. 3 months is still 3 months, to the mind, no matter if you learn for 5 minutes a day or 5 hours.

The more time you invest in this period, the more you learn. The more you learn, the easier it will be to look back and not see wasted time.

## Mezasu.com

Most people don't put in the hours, then quit, because they believe they can't learn languages.

The Language Learner's Pocketbook

# **The Four Phases of Learning**

1. Comprehension

2. Understanding

3. Reproduction

4. Automatic Reproduction

---

I needed a way to structure the learning process so I could better learn vocabulary. These are the phases I came up with.

Context example used: Math Class.

# **Comprehension**

This is the first encounter; the "Potential" for understanding.

We've all sat through math classes before. You enter the room and prepare yourself for the mind numbing lesson that's about to take place...well, at least if you can stay awake during them.

This phase starts when the teacher first throws the concepts at you: The first link.

You may comprehend what is said, but that doesn't mean you understand it; yet. You may hear it multiple times and still not get it. Each time is another link that adds to your potential to understand.

You can ask questions, get different opinions, or look for situations in your life; anything to piece together what you learn.

## **Understanding**

You earn the ability to recognize what you're looking at. You know how it works and can perform it in assisted isolation.

To move through understanding you must review what you have come across.

# The Language Learner's Pocketbook

Just because you can understand, doesn't mean you have competence.

At this point, you are still in the lesson. You continue to ask questions and do example problems until you can do them without assistance. This is where you can focus your energy on one problem at a time; isolated practice. You don't have to be correct 100% of the time. If you get in the ballpark, you're doing fine.

## **Reproduction**

You can perform without assistance in isolation or with assistance in real world situations.

This is your math homework. You are still practicing in isolation; though, you now work with a range of problems. You learn to determine which formula goes to which problem and how to come to the right solution.

This leads to the math test where you get placed in front of a set problems: no guide, no assistance. This is a glimpse into automatic reproduction, but you're not there, yet.

## **Automatic Reproduction**

You need no assistance and have the ability to perform within seconds of encountering a problem.

This is where the mathematician goes and gets a job; let's say an engineer.

The engineer's job is to start with the problem, diagnose a solution, then work to reach a conclusion. They may even know how to instantly solve a problem due to years of experience. The only way to get here is by extensive practice.

---

That is how the four phases work. Can you already imagine a way to use these in language learning?

# The Language Learner's Pocketbook

For how I apply these, refer to, "Vocabulary in the Four Phases" in the Game Plan section of this book, but before you go there...Let's talk about funnels!

# **Focus Funnels**

The amount of parts in language learning could leave you overwhelmed. Grammar, vocabulary, listening, reading, speaking, and whatever else is unique to the language.

It can start out fun, discovering reason within the chaos, but that fun could turn into resentment when packed to the brim. If you don't maintain your focus, it might take you months to master a basic concept.

This is where the Funnels come in. Each skill is a different funnel which fills your container of understanding.

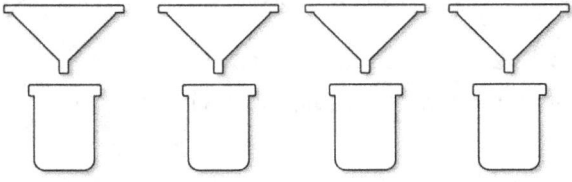

When you pour into a funnel, the first bit can go through in an instant. As you add more

# The Language Learner's Pocketbook

and more, the funnel will get backed up. If you add too much, the funnel will overflow.

On the other side, if you try to fill ten funnels at once, you will lose a lot of information before it has a chance of entering.

There are times where adding in bulk makes sense, but with whole language learning this is not the case. There is too much to go through to add everything all at once.

From the first moment you pour, you begin the Comprehension phase. To get through understanding, you must review and review until it comes through the funnel.

If you stop reviewing, it's like pouring into a funnel that is aimed away from the container.

Add new concepts; then review, review, review. As you're reviewing, you fill the next funnel.

# Mezasu.com

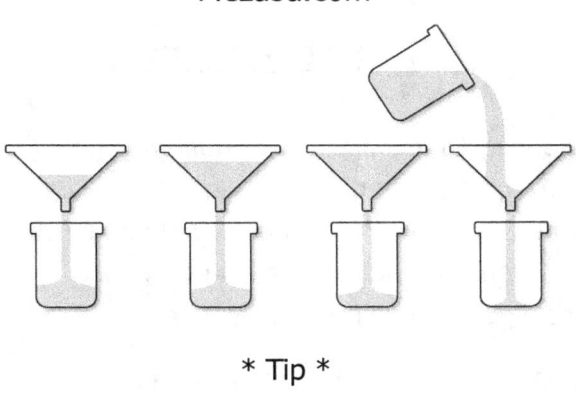

* Tip *

---

It wouldn't be smart to do one individual concept at a time. It will take too long. Take grammar, for example, it likes to flow together. What you learn now will come up again at different times. So it is best to learn in groups and review those groups.

* Notice *

---

This concept is to structure your thoughts so you don't overwork yourself. Sometimes you will have to fill multiple containers at the same time. You want your time to be effective. If you do too many things at once, you will get exhausted.

The Language Learner's Pocketbook

# **Wall Measuring**

It's easy to feel like you've gone nowhere through months of study; when, in reality, you progressed more than you think. Most people leave themselves with no way to distinguish the difference from before.

Bring back your childhood obsession: Measuring! If you weren't obsessed about your height, you were a rare one.

Height is everything to a kid. Every millimeter counts one step closer to adulthood or at least to go on the amusement park rides.

You may have measured yourself on a weekly basis, maybe daily. You wanted to know how much you've grown, even if it was only a millimeter.

Grab your tape measure and a pencil and start measuring!

You should have a monthly check up to test your performance. Do the same task each time. It could be a writing or speaking prompt. Anything that will show your current, raw skill level.

No preparation, just doing.

That way you can look back to see how much you have improved from a month ago. It will be bitter sweet to compare and contrast, but you will feel much better about your current situation. You will get motivated because you can see/hear your progress.

The Language Learner's Pocketbook

# **Habit for Language Learning**

You may hate me for saying this but…

Active Language Study CANNOT become a habit!

There is too much of a mental hurdle to get started and even more to continue. Habits are things you do to the point where you don't think about them anymore.

Just because you can do something every day does not make it a habit. Eating is not necessarily a habit. Take it from a guy who forgets to eat, but I do eat every day.

Same goes for working out. You can do it every day but, as you know, missing only one day could set you on a path of not working out for months.

This isn't to say you can't build habits to grow the DESIRE to learn languages (or to work out).

Let me use working out as an example because we have all done it at some point.

In the morning:

- Get up and drink a cup of water.
- Do your normal routine (Ex. brushing your teeth, getting dressed, etc.)
- Make something healthy to eat (Ex. fruit smoothie, omelet, etc.)
- Pack your gym bag and take it with you.

During the day:

- Make small choices that promote a healthy diet (Ex. change ice cream to yogurt).
- You can opt for a standing desk.
- When taking a break, take a walk around the block.

By the time you go to work out, you have conditioned your brain to think healthy all day.

# The Language Learner's Pocketbook

The mind is strong when trying to maintain consistency. To match your previous actions, you will choose more of the same actions to support your decision.

Now to apply this to language learning.

In the morning:

- Wake up and add one new word. During your routine you can build connections or stories around it. (I will explain building connections later).

During the day:

- Switch off your music and tune into the language. Don't worry if you don't understand.

- When you have a spare moment, review the words you have added.

- Fill the empty periods with something in the language. (Ex. audio in the background)

That's not much to do, right? And it does what it needs to. It conditions the brain to think about the language before you sit down to do the hardest task. You may even get so excited that you run home to study!

How long does it take to build habits?

You may have heard 21 days, but that is only the minimum. These are activities that are the easiest to do, like drinking water in the morning.

The average time for building a habit is around 66 days with the range being anywhere from 18 to 254 days.

The more difficult the habit, the longer it will take to accomplish. (Ex. changing your diet).

Account for these numbers and the difficulty of the habit you want to build. That way you don't quit before you make them.

Add your own personal touch. Create your own habits that are simple to do and grow your desire to learn.

# Language Learning Methods

# **Preface of Language Learning Methods**

Now, we can get into the meat and bones of language learning: the methods you will use to get proficient.

These are the building blocks. They aren't the "end-all-be-all" approach to learning. This section is to introduce you to various concepts about language learning and is designed as a crash course. So don't expect that every single detail will be laid out for you.

For more of a road map, go to the Game Plan section of this book. I will use these concepts to lay out what I would do when starting a language.

You can always take these concepts and develop your own style. Nothing is set in stone; and, in the end, the time invested in active study time is the most important part.

# The Language Learner's Pocketbook

# **Spaced Repetition**

The Spaced Repetition System (SRS) is one of the most widely used tools in language learning.

Memories fade over time. The first occurrence will fade quickly so a review will be necessary soon after; as to not forget it. Each review increases the potential for it to stay in your long term memory.

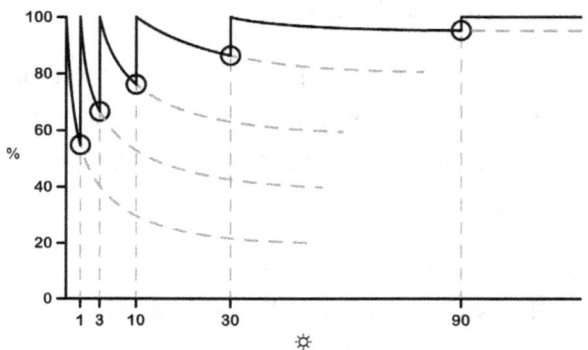

\* The chart shows the retention percentage over a given amount of days. The circles pinpoint the time of review.

# Mezasu.com

The Interval (time in between each review) increases after each review.

It is a good rule of thumb to have the intervals increase by 2-3x from the previous duration for every correct answer.

To handle incorrect answers, you can use one of two different methods, shown below.

Type 1:

For each correct answer, you increase the duration of the next review. For every wrong answer, you revert it back to the previous duration.

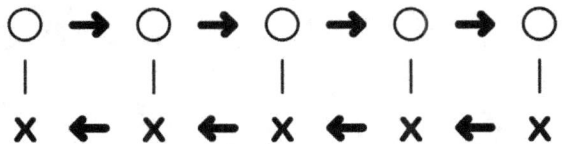

Type 2:

Same for correct answers. However, on incorrect answers, you restart all the way from the beginning.

# The Language Learner's Pocketbook

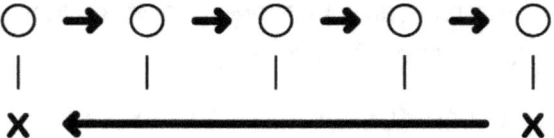

Type two is a bit more stressful to do because it could cause backups in your reviews. I don't recommend it as is, but if you prefer it, do what works best for you.

In a future section, I will go through my personal way of using SRS to learn Vocabulary. It is different compared to other tools out there, but I have found it to be the most effective for me.

# **Mastering Vocabulary**

When adding vocabulary, it is tempting to take as many words as you can and hope for the best. Some programs use this to get you in. It's like a candy store. You walk in, you grab all the candy you can get your hands on, and the next thing you know, someone is patting your back as you're face deep in a toilet bowl.

With so many new words to learn, what can you do to give yourself the best step forward?

## **Connections**

When you get a new word, the first step you need to do is to connect back to anything you already know.

The connections could be rough; but, as long as you make the effort to build connections, you form a stronger bond with the word...

# The Language Learner's Pocketbook

rather than massacring candy and hoping it stays in.

As an example, I'll use the Spanish word, Galletas (cookies).

You can easily imagine a cookie. Better yet, have a cookie right in your hand so you can take in everything.

- Images
- Smells
- Touch
- Emotions
- Etc.

Now take the sounds of the word. Try to connect the sounds back to something you already know. I made the phrase, "The girl let us have cookies".

Close your eyes and see this happening. The key part is, "Girl let us". (Galletas)

Can you see the connection? It doesn't have to be exact. It only has to trigger the memory.

Knowing the rules of pronunciation are important. That way you don't mess up with loose connections.

This is one of the most important steps that most people…including myself…never did when they started.

If you brute force everything like I did, your vocabulary will suffer. When I figured out what I had done wrong, it was easier for me to start over from step one.

## **Mnemonics**

Mnemonics are an extension of the concept above.

Some popular mnemonics:
- Every Good Boy Deserves Fudge
- ROY G. BIV
- Columbus sailed the ocean blue; In fourteen hundred ninety-two

You can even use real images to assist you.

I do have to warn against the use of connections created by a 3rd-party.

Creating the connection is part of the learning process. The time and effort you spend creating one will better aid your memory.

If you have no options left and you find one that is so good you'll never forget it, by all means use it. But this is a final option, never the first.

## **Memory Palaces**

This is an effective yet time consuming method.

For each word you want to learn, connect it to the location, then build a story around it. This is similar to how we made connections earlier. You should use rooms you have been in before, and can visualize, while creating your own.

I created a model of a kitchen to give you a brief introduction to memory palaces.

You walk in from the top and make your way around the numbers 1 – 5.

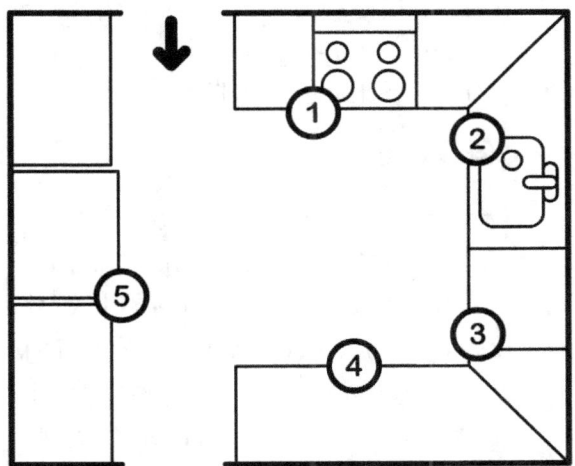

1. Stove

   We could think back to the cookies example and imagine a beautiful girl letting us eat the [cookies] she pulled fresh out of the oven. Take in the smells and the texture. Then take a nice big bite and feel the cookie melt in your mouth. Don't forget to thank the (girl) who (let us) have some cookies!

# The Language Learner's Pocketbook

2. Sink

   You could learn the word to [wash] or [clean]. The sink is an easy pick for this. Scrub those plates sparkly clean with your soap that smells like raspberries.

3. Dishwasher

   Another cleaning tool, but this one is a [machine] and you can hear all the moving parts from the other side of the house. Or you can apply it to [loading/packing], trying to fit every last dish in so you don't have to wash anything by hand.

4. Countertop

   Where you cook or eat. This place could get messy. [Stain] is a good word you can learn. There's a big old stain from the wine you spilled from the failed romantic night...embarrassing!

5. Refrigerator

## Mezasu.com

The fridge is a good place to preserve food, but it's not a fool proof way. Maybe you went away on vacation and came back to find all of your food [rotting] away. The stench is so bad it's easier to toss the fridge and get a new one.

Pick any room, any object, create any story, and you can build a strong connection to the words that you try to learn. Your limit is your imagination.

### * Tip *

---

The weirder the stories, the easier they are to remember. Make them as graphic as possible. You may feel strange in the process of making them, "What if my friends and family see this? What would they think of me?" Don't let that stop you! This is for learning. If you don't feel weird about telling friends or family, they may not be graphic enough (or you have a high tolerance for weird situations).

---

The Language Learner's Pocketbook

# **Vocabulary in Context**

The absolute best way to internalize vocabulary is to put it into real context. Meaning you should take every word you learn and put it in real sentences as quickly as possible.

Many words could have the same general meaning, but have different connotations.

Ex. Pero – Sino (Spanish) | Meaning: But

The way to understand the distinction is to see how each word is used. You'll never get that association if you only practice the words in isolation.

However, I do believe in slight isolation when adding vocabulary. Start with the process explained above and practice recalling the words using those connections.

Once you can recognize these words in isolation, you move them into sentences.

Mezasu.com

# **What You Know +1**

In theory, you should know 100% of the sentences you find; what you know +1.

Your +1 is the word you have studied. At this point, you should have a basic idea of the meaning. All other words should be known.

Ergo the 100%.

Don't use any sentence that has a new word. There is no point in trying to wrap your head around a random word that you have not studied or have no intention of studying.

This improves what you know and allows you to focus on one word.

* Notice *

---

Don't feel like you can't pick up a book and read it if you don't know all of the words on the page. This +1 concept is for when you're learning and reviewing vocabulary.

---

The Language Learner's Pocketbook

## **Passive Learning**

There is also a passive approach to learning vocabulary. I would recommend this for items that don't play a major role in the language, but may be useful.

Ex. animals, foods, objects, etc.

Here's how it goes:

Write a list of 25 words with the meaning next to it.

You're done!

...well, at least for the next 2 weeks.

* Note *

---

Make sure you physically write them. That is part of the process.

---

After two weeks, come back and mark off all the words you can remember.

If you can remember the word, you know it. (However, be sure to apply these words. If you don't use them, you lose them.)

Now, create a second list with all the words you didn't remember. Let those sit for another two weeks.

When the time comes, repeat.

Do this at least once more.

From here you have multiple options.

- You can keep going until the list hits zero.
- You can move the left over words to a more active approach.
- You can refresh the list filling it back to 25 (Ex. you had 7 words left so you add 18 to equal 25).

This is a go-with-the-flow method, which is why I would recommend it for words that don't play a major role in the language.

The Language Learner's Pocketbook

# **Mastering Grammar**

Everyone has mixed feelings about grammar. You either love it or hate it.

Some will say you don't have to study it. I don't agree with that. Trust me, I've been to the dark side and well…it's dark there.

No matter how you feel, you have to study it because it shines light on the language.

Look at grammar as if you were trying to build a house. You want to build it for security so you can keep all the residents, the furniture, utilities, etc. safe inside.

Grammar provides the foundation and structure to keep the words safe.

If you try to build a house only by analyzing other houses, you will only gather a few pieces to the puzzle; but, there will be a lot which remains invisible.

You can trial-and-error your way, but that will take time.

To build the foundation of a house, you need concrete. If you had concrete, I'm sure you could figure out how to pour and level it after some tests, but we don't have concrete here. We have to learn how to make it ourselves. Do you know how concrete is made so it stays solid and doesn't crumble?

We're not making a house out of sticks and mud. Even then, that would require complex ideas that need to be taught if you want to apply them in a reasonable amount of time.

Don't waste your time figuring it out by yourself. You will learn faster and better with instruction.

## **Writing, Writing, and More Writing**

In this digital world, you might think, "Well, I'm never going to write the language by hand anyway...as long as I can read and type, I should be fine, right?"

# The Language Learner's Pocketbook

...Maybe? But why take the chance.

Writing by hand takes both mental and physical energy. It's time consuming, which is why it's so useful and is also what turns people away from it.

The time it takes to write allows your mind to become aware of the pieces built into each sentence and each word. The movement of writing forms another link which aids what you learn.

Reading only takes mental energy and our brains are notoriously lazy. We could skip over words without realizing it, which would leave gaps in our understanding.

Passive vocabulary, for example. You can see it and understand it, but when it comes time to use it, you don't know how to. Reading alone won't bring these to active status.

You need active study and writing is one of the best ways to do that.

Find good textbooks (plural) and write everything multiple times over.

I used to hate textbooks. It never felt as if there was enough. Not enough explanations, not enough practice, not enough anything. I was left in a state of confusion, which made me frustrated. Once my mind quit, I would start to look up all the answers in the back of the book and lie to myself that it's still practice.

I have updated my feelings toward textbooks with one simple idea:

---

The exercises aren't the homework, they are the test.

---

Your homework comes from writing and reviewing the example sentences over and over again, until they are drilled into your head. Only after you do your homework, should you take the test.

This constant writing and review leads into another core concept...

# The Language Learner's Pocketbook

## **Over-Learning**

We're not here to learn like we did in school. This isn't to cram for a test, then mind dump everything. You are here to gain actual competence.

To become a master, you must repeat the process until it becomes redundant; until it becomes instinct.

---

"I fear not the man who has practiced 10,000 kicks once, but I fear the man who has practiced one kick 10,000 times." – Bruce Lee

---

How much have you read, written, and listened to your native language over the years?

In language learning, your goal is to condense those years into a shorter period of time. For a native speaker to become fluent it takes, on average, until the age eight. What if you can cut that in half?

Write, Write, Write! Once it's redundant, write more.

Focus on one sentence at a time. Write and repeat.

As your skills improve, you will start to form paragraphs. It will look like a child wrote it, but it is the key to develop more complex writing, and therefore speaking, in the future.

---

Ex. I like food. The food looks good. The smell is nice. I eat the food. It tastes delicious. I want dessert. Now, I'm full. My stomach hurts. I have no regrets.

The Language Learner's Pocketbook

# **Mastering Listening**

We're going to use the same concepts of condensing and over-learning here as well.

## **Over-Listening**

To do this, you will need a good audio file that comes with the transcript of everything said.

Take no more than 5 minutes at a time.

Start by listening to the audio file 3 times without reading along or pausing. Your goal is to understand as much as possible in real time (you can't pause people in the physical world).

Each time, you build off of what you missed the last time. Little by little, you will piece together what you know.

After, you will do the same while reading along. This will help you recognize words you know visually, but haven't picked up in audio.

This will also solidify and/or correct what you have heard before.

Next, dissect the entire transcript. Read it and look up any and all words you don't know. Make a list of them with their meaning. This will be your "Cheat Sheet" later.

You don't have to study them all, but for this practice you should have an understanding of what they mean during the session. This will help you to distinguish words (and who knows, you might learn it).

If there is any grammar you don't understand, try to find an answer and write the reason why.

Listen to the audio again; 3 more times. (Only use the cheat sheet, no reading).

If you haven't taken a break at this point, you're going to want to because the next part is...

Write, Write, Write!

# The Language Learner's Pocketbook

I want you to write the whole transcript and the translation at least 5 times, if not more.

Then, listen 3 more times: no reading; no cheat sheet.

With that...You are done!

Depending on your daily study time, you may want to split this into 2 or 3 days.

This is a long and involved process, but you will come out much better in the end. Not only will this help you with listening, it will help with grammar and vocabulary, too.

I would not recommend this for beginners. This is an advanced method and you should have an intermediate level of understanding before trying this.

However, if you find a [good] source for beginner level audio, go ahead and use it.

# **What is Good Audio?**

NEVER determine whether the audio is good based off of how well you understand it. When you're just starting, the only way you will understand is if the speech is slowed down because you haven't built the tools to understand natural paced audio raw.

While slow audio may be a confidence boost in the short-term, it has bad long-term effects for two main reasons:

1. The Sounds Are Not Natural

    When a speaker speaks slowly they have a natural tendency to pronounce words more sharply. This is good for understanding; but in natural speech, words get chopped and mashed together.

    "How are you doing?" turns into, "Howyadoin'"

# The Language Learner's Pocketbook

You get your mind used to listening to sounds that will never be made during natural encounters.

2. Slow Reaction time

You can't practice for the sprint by jogging.

When native speakers speak, they're going for the sprint. They get their message across as quickly as possible. Slow audio forces your mind to react slowly. This could leave you in a daze with even the most basic sentences.

Always get audio that is at a natural speaking rate. ALWAYS!!!

# **Mastering Pronunciation**

This is the last piece to the puzzle and could come naturally during your studies, but only partly.

The goal is to sound as natural as possible. We may never get the native-like qualities for every single detail, but we can aim for it.

---

Aim for the moon to reach the clouds.

---

Practicing pronunciation is the easiest to explain because there is only one way of doing it. Mimic everything!

You did it as a child and you still do it today. If you hear a joke and you want to share it with your friends, you will mimic the person who told the joke.

You will either capture the essence of the speaker or you will be left with chirping crickets, while saying, "Well, it was funnier when they said it."

# The Language Learner's Pocketbook

You don't want crickets in language learning so you must practice by mimicking.

## **The Musician Method**

Learn proper pronunciation through the same methods musicians use to learn new and difficult pieces of music.

All music has beats per minute (BPM) to set the pace of the music. Most modern music sticks to one steady BPM; though, if you look at any classical music, you will find songs where the BPM changes in the middle.

You can change the feel of the same music by speeding up or slowing down the pace. As you change the rate, you also change the difficulty.

During practice, you will never start at full speed. You will struggle to keep up and you will develop bad habits that could lead to sloppy sounds.

Pick one sentence you wish to practice. Here, you're going to need a tool that could clip, alter, and record audio.

Isolate the one sentence and try to mimic it at full speed.

Be sure to record yourself and compare. What you say might come out much different than what you think.

If you're able to copy it perfectly and consistently at full speed (multiple times), then keep on copying it. Over-learning!

Throughout the day, you can repeat that sentence to yourself as you practiced.

If you can't, you need to slow down the audio so you can hear what is happening.

* Tip *

---

You can slow down audio of someone talking normally, however, you can never speed up audio of someone talking slowly.

---

# The Language Learner's Pocketbook

## * Warning *

---

As you slow down audio, you distort the sounds. Don't go too far or you will lose the natural sounds you want to replicate. The point is to hear all the small sounds and alterations.

Rather than hearing, "Howyadoin'" at full pace, you slow it down enough to hear where it cuts and meshes. "How-ya-doin'".

---

Copy the speed until you become confident. If you still struggle to copy it with your mouth, you can slow your speech even further.

The point of this exercise is for perfect control.

Control it slow, then speed up until you reach a natural pace. If you speed up too fast and lose control, don't worry. Slow it back down and regain control.

After you get up to a normal speed, Repetition is Key!

Keep saying it to yourself even if you're out in public. If you have a chance to use it during a real conversation, use it.

Use it or lose it.

# The Game Plan

# **Preface of the Game Plan**

As it stands, if someone came to me and asked how to start learning a language, this section is how I would guide them.

I add new concepts not mentioned in the previous sections for two reasons:

---

Either, they are unique to the language and require distinct instruction...

Or they are based on my personal interests. More like helpful tips than official methods.

---

If you are new to learning, I recommend that you stick to this outline. Since this isn't the only path you can take, you might feel the need to search for the optimum method.

There is no optimum method.

No matter if you have the best or worst methods, those with the most invested time are the ones with the greatest results.

Stop searching and put in the time!

The Language Learner's Pocketbook

# **Overview**

Here is a quick guide of what is in this section. The times given are based off of the study time (per day) of 1 to 2 hours. The ones without times could be done indefinitely and at the individual's discretion.

1. Phonetics (& Writing System) (1 week max)

2. Beginner Level Textbook (3 - 6 weeks)

3. Four More Textbooks (1 month+ each)

4. Vocabulary in the Four Phases

5. Listening & Advanced Study

6. Speaking & Pronunciation

Mezasu.com

# **The Game Plan**

## **Phonetics (& Writing System)**

You can't understand the language if you don't understand the sounds.

Each language has a complex set of sounds, some of which you have never made before. They may, also, be paired with a different writing system.

These two go hand-in-hand.

Take Japanese, for example, notorious for its complex writing system. There are three main scripts and one nonstandard way.

1. Hiragana

This is the main alphabet. They account for all the sounds in the language. You can write anything with Hiragana alone. (Ex. あ、い、う、え、お | か、き、く、け、こ | etc.)

# The Language Learner's Pocketbook

2. Katakana

The same sounds written in a different style. Used for loan-words or stylistic choice. (Ex. ア、イ、ウ、エ、オ | カ、キ、ク、ケ、コ | etc.)

3. Kanji

Chinese characters used in place of Hiragana to give meaning and structure to the sentences. (Ex. 犬、食、好、何、etc.)

4. Romaji (nonstandard)

This is an approximation of how the Japanese language would be written using the Roman Script as the base. (Ex. Inu, Shoku, Kō, Nani, etc.)

You'll never see Romaji used unless you're trying to translate names or places. However, many Japanese learners will choose to start here, due to the complex nature of the writing. It can bridge the gap, but if you stick with it too long it will be harder in the long run.

匂い and 臭い can, both, be read as Nioi (Knee-oh-ee). They both mean smell.

The difference comes with the Kanji used in the word.

(匂) Gives a meaning of fragrant.

(臭) Gives a meaning of stinking.

One is positive, the other is negative, and you would never be able to tell the difference if you used Romaji.

This is one of the many examples that show how the writing system helps give meaning in ways that could only be found if you know it. It also opens you up to the world of content in the language. No one is going to translate everything for you.

Before you ask, "Are you expecting me to learn the entire writing system within a week?!" No! But you can understand the basic functions in a week.

Mastering is different from understanding.

# The Language Learner's Pocketbook

Context is everything! Seeing and practicing the real language will give you plenty of natural training in phonetics and the writing system.

Understand how it works, then jump in!

## **Beginner Level Textbook**

As a self-studier, one of the most valuable tools you have is a textbook.

I know many people wonder if there are free options that could take the place of this and, as far as I've seen, it's rare to find one that would be worth your time.

If you're serious about language learning, be prepared to spend money. Trust me…I tried the free method for years and got nowhere.

With the textbook, the task is simple; follow the concepts talked about in the Mastering Grammar section.

Do not try to power through the book. Write! No shortcuts. Write! No skipping. Write! No worrying about how much you have left to go. Just Write!

One book could take you more than a month to complete, and that is fine. We are here to "Know", not just "Understand".

Be sure to find a book with good structure. Even books in the same company and same branding could be very different in the content it offers.

In my experience of learning Spanish and Japanese, I got two basic textbooks from the same company and branding. I enjoyed the Japanese book which I got first, so I decided to get the Spanish book as well.

The Spanish book is one of the worst I've seen! There were no explanations for anything. It throws you in and hopes for the best. It could've been fine if it was marketed as a review book; but this was targeted to beginners which is when explanations mean everything.

Know how the book is set up before you buy it.

## **Four More Textbooks**

Line up four more textbooks at varying levels. You can always do more, but I recommend a minimum of 5 books total.

This will give you plenty of time to cover the major parts of the language and, also, get you into intermediate level territory.

That said, the books aren't enough to secure an intermediate level. Vocabulary is an important piece to the puzzle and textbooks will only teach a small collection of words.

## **Vocabulary in the Four Phases**

You set your vocabulary goals at the beginning of this book, right?

If you don't have your numbers counted, this is the time to go back and calculate them.

I have a unique approach to learning vocabulary so I want to explain one concept before I get into the meat of it.

## **The Filing System**

In our native language we all have a filing system. Words we know, words we recognize and words we have seen, but don't understand.

We have spent years building and organizing this system.

Our job is to replicate the system the best we can in our new language.

\* The Catch \*

---

You can't file what you have never seen…and you can't recall what you have never filed.

---

# The Language Learner's Pocketbook

This means, if you run into a word in the wild, you have no way of recognizing what is in front of you.

You must get it filed, at least, once.

Here is the only time I will recommend you go for bulk. Add more than you think you should; add more than you may be able to manage. Don't worry if they don't click in your head. Keep them in review until they do.

This isn't perfection; we're filing.

We want to condense the amount of words we have seen into a short period of time. This way, if we run into them, we already have a link. Get them in, then rely on natural progression to finish off the job.

Start with a frequency list. This is the quickest way to get the most useful vocabulary.

# Mezasu.com

## What is a Frequency list?

---

These lists have compiled thousands of written sources to find which words appear the most.

There are flaws to these lists.

Since it is difficult to replicate with the spoken word, you will find some words that serve no purpose in the spoken language.

These may include technical words or complex words used in writing.

You will also come across different variations of the same word.

However, I will add these anyway. You never know when a word will be useful. If it's filed, you can recall it.

---

I want you to think of the review for vocabulary, not as practice, but as scrolling through an index. We file the words we recognize and mark them as known. Then move them into a greater phase.

# The Language Learner's Pocketbook

While you do the textbooks, you will find many of these words. This is the natural practice you need. When it shows in the lesson, you may finally connect a word that you have only seen in your system and you have struggled to understand.

That's the magic of the filing system.

Now onto the phases!

## **Comprehension**

This is all about connections! (Go back to Mastering Vocabulary / Connections to get the overview of what we're doing here.)

I always start with a frequency list. It's effective and you never have to worry about searching for words because you have a master list. You can always drop in words when you see fit.

I aim for 25 words per day, but you can stick to the number you calculated before.

This is where we make the connections.

# Mezasu.com

Remember the word Galletas? Repeat that process for each word and drop them in!

"Drop them into what?" you might ask. It's our handy dandy Spaced Repetition Tool!

This tool works like a flashcard system. You have a front side of what you wish to study and a back side that gives you the answer.

## Format of Cards

---

Front Side – The translation of the word (native language).

Back Side – The word (target language).

---

This is isolated practice. We are not training for recognition here. We are training for memory. This is why your native language is on the front. You want to practice recalling the words with no help other than your connections.

There is one issue that will arise. These review sessions could get tedious with bulk

# The Language Learner's Pocketbook

additions. As you know, not every word will stick into your mind.

If you constantly refresh the intervals of the words, you will clog your reviews. This will leave you frustrated when you see the same words daily and feel no closer to learning them.

With this in mind, I made a workaround to allow you to push through without the constant backup.

I like to call it the Progressive Spaced Repetition System (P-SRS).

Don't restart every word as you get them wrong; rather, allow the words to progress within a range of intervals. Only when the word has reached (or passed) the peak interval will the word be reset.

This reduces the stagnation and strain on your brain from having the same frustrating words show on a daily basis.

For vocabulary, set the peak interval of one week. When you get here, you have two choices:

1. If wrong, reset it and start the process again.

2. If correct, you will move that word onto the next phase.

Two more situations that might happen when you get it wrong:

1. You were partially correct – In this case, you may need extra time with the word, so you will reset it. | Or you may lack the context, in which case, you should push it through to the next phase anyway.

2. You were completely wrong - I would recommend that you revisit the connection; if it isn't strong enough, make a new one.

Repeat until you can pass the word.

# The Language Learner's Pocketbook

## **Understanding**

After you build the word in isolation, you have to give it context.

The process is simple:

Find, at least, 3 sentences which use that word. Then review.

### Format of Cards

---

Front Side – the sentence in your target language.

Back Side – the translation (if you have audio, put that here, not in the front).

---

This is where we train for recognition. Can you read and understand the sentence?

The target interval, for testing out, is 3 months. For the reset interval, have a rate of one month maximum.

Mezasu.com

* Important *

---

Use +1 when finding sentences for review (refer to "What You Know +1").

---

## **Reproduction**

Once you have tested out, you have two options:

1. Apply in Real Context - If you apply what you learn, you don't have to do anymore SRS review for the sentence. (Real contexts can include textbook practice, attempting to speak to native speakers, etc.)

2. Not Applied in Context - If you can't apply it, you need remedial practice. If you don't use it; you lose it.

You should always strive for 'in-context' practice. But sometimes it's not possible; in which case, you can continue the training by flipping the same sentence cards as before.

# The Language Learner's Pocketbook

## Format of Cards

---

Front Side – the translation (native language).

Back Side – the example sentence in your target language (keep the audio here).

---

This will give you time to re-create the language in your mind.

Some people say you should avoid translation, but you can actually use it to your benefit here.

By translating back and forth between the languages, you build stronger connections.

Where translation goes wrong is when you rely on translation to do the work for you. Here you're training your mind to switch between the languages.

Once completed, you're done with the review for that sentence.

Now, you may be wondering, "Why do we stop reviewing the cards?"

Allow me to explain why it's better to end rather than continue to build the intervals.

Our brains are masters at picking out patterns. These cards are the same each time and the brain picks up on that, they become patterns. At that time, you respond off of pattern rather than actual competence.

This is why it is best to practice in varying real-world contexts. Translating from your native language to the target language is a different skill than responding in real-time.

Always strive for practice in-context.

## **Automatic Reproduction**

This one is simple: Use it – Use it – Use it!

The only way to build the muscle of automatically reproducing the language is to use the language.

You can also go back to the Mastering Grammar / Over-Learning section to see how to do this without relying on the presence of a native speaker. But, as you would guess, practice in-context is best.

---

That concludes how I use the four phases in learning vocabulary.

This has been the most effective method for me because it allows for a large amount of words to be added in a short period of time and give them context.

The context is what most people forget.

# **Listening & Advanced Study**

During your time with the textbooks, you should listen to a lot of native level content, not for the purpose of understanding, but to adapt your ears to the sounds.

After the five books and thousands of words later, you will be able to handle heavier study methods and have a basic ability to distinguish the sounds made.

Go back to Mastering Listening for an outline of what you will be doing here.

It is important to find a source of audio you won't mind listening to over and over.

If there's a voice which annoys you, do not continue. You will hate it, which will distract you from paying attention to the language.

This method can be continued indefinitely as there is a never ending supply of content to choose from at various different levels.

# The Language Learner's Pocketbook

If you watch a show for this practice, I would recommend watching the whole show once through beforehand. (You can use subtitles if you want).

You should have already enjoyed the show. This way you won't worry about the plot and you can focus on learning.

As a reward, after studying each episode, you can watch the full episode and even the full season again while gaining a high level of understanding without the need of subtitles.

## **Speaking & Pronunciation**

This is the most difficult part - the step into why you started in the first place: to speak the language.

It is a new difficult world to jump into. The change could make your mind run wild, "Did I say that right? Was that the proper word? Do they even understand me?"

Breathe; relax.

You never have to jump in if you don't want to. Some will recommend you speak from day one, you don't have to. There will be benefits to this, but it's not for everyone. Others will tell you to wait until you have reached a certain level before you start. This might take years to build to and isn't for everyone, as well.

These are the two extreme ideologies and each side has its own positives and negatives. These serve to fit the individual's personal style of learning.

Which one do you believe will be a better fit for you?

### Speak from Day One

Ideology

Break through the barrier most people have when learning a language. Throw away the excuse and fear of messing up. Embrace the mistakes because that is how you know you are making progress. Language is all

# The Language Learner's Pocketbook

about communication so get out there and communicate.

## Positives

Gets you comfortable with the idea of making mistakes. This will help you not shy away from opportunities when they appear.

Gives you instant satisfaction when a task is accomplished in the language and will serve as a motivation boost.

## Negatives

There will be a lot of mistakes and you will struggle to speak. This could lead to unnecessary stress.

May force you to say something you know is wrong while never getting the correct way to say it.

# Mezasu.com

## Speak After Lots of Study

### Ideology

You should never speak unless you know it is correct so you don't build bad habits. Aim to sound like an educated native speaker. Seek perfect understanding and quick responses.

### Positives

Gives you time for perfect practice so you know that you will speak with correct words and proper grammar.

Doesn't force you to invent new sentences which may be wrong.

### Negatives

Can lead to perfectionism which will cause stress when making errors.

Takes a long time and could feel like you go months without any progress. Some might quit before trying to speak.

# The Language Learner's Pocketbook

Again, these are the two extremes.

On one side, you have the people who strive for simple communication; on the other side, you have the people who strive for absolute fluency.

Most people won't fit into the extremes and I don't either. I recommend a mix.

You should get some early communication with a native speaker, but I would not force it past simple messaging. Don't worry about calling or voice messaging, yet. You won't be ready for it.

With messaging, you get some benefits of the early start while lightening its down side. You won't be forced to strain yourself with on-the-spot answers. It gives you time to think, search, and create proper sentences with the knowledge that you are building.

There are various places online where you can find an exchange partner, but a good partner could take time to find.

You want someone who you enjoy talking to and is willing to help you. There will be some who only want to help themselves. They're annoying and you should avoid turning into one as well.

During this time, you will have to translate often. At this stage, you aren't going for perfect use. You should focus on building a personal connection, become friends, and then worry about the language.

* Meaning *

---

Don't bombard them with questions. They aren't your encyclopedia. They're a person with a life and they're not going to work for you for free.

Helpful tip: Don't be over friendly and try to help the person with every single detail. It may be helpful, but it gets annoying because your conversations will revolve around everything they do wrong.

---

# The Language Learner's Pocketbook

Meanwhile, you will be doing the real practice. Go through everything I have talked about in this book. You will find that your conversations will progress over time. This is a simple way to track your improvement.

At some point, you will be ready for a live call. The first one can be rough. It's a good idea to have a plan ahead of time. (Ex. conversation starters to break silent moments and pre-written responses to fall back on…just in case your brain stops working for whatever reason).

Before you make your first live call, I would recommend doing some dedicated listening and speaking practice.

You don't have to go into the same detail I talked about in the Mastering Listening and Pronunciation sections of this book, but doing some will allow you to build confidence in what you're doing.

You could simply repeat what you practiced. This way, you can have native ears to hear and fix any inconsistencies. However, don't rely on live calls alone to fix these mistakes. It's easy to brush off errors if they are abundant in your speech.

For each and every live call, your practice should be, at least, ten times the duration of the call. This is where the perfectionist side comes into play. The more perfect practice you have, the more comfortable you will feel. Practice to the point where you don't have to think about it anymore.

As you progress, be kind and help out; you can make a great new friend out of that exchange partner. The added bonus of a native friend is that you can have a tour guide if you were to travel to the country. They will be able to show you the places that only the locals would know. (Of course, you should return the favor as well).

# Parting Information

# **Preface to Parting Information**

There are a few more bits of information I would like to cover. They didn't fit into the rest of the book, but they are important for you to understand. They can help you in your learning and, also, clear some misconceptions.

The Language Learner's Pocketbook

# **Culture**

When you learn a language, you also learn their culture.

Even if the outward appearance seems familiar, the culture can be different.

For example, Japan, on the surface can look like an Americanized country, but their culture is different to that of the U.S.

The biggest difference is the politeness level. There's a hierarchical system of politeness which spreads out through the whole country. The U.S. has no cultural politeness system, for better or worse.

The most interesting part is that Japan's politeness is built into the language. The swear words you know and love don't exist in the language. To insult someone, you simply reduce the politeness of your speech.

This is important to know because you can insult everyone you talk to without realizing it. Culture is important!

# **Money Motivation**

Money can be a big motivator in learning a language. This is why English has become such a globally recognized language. It is highly used in business and the internet. Many people who learn English do so for employment.

I started to learn Spanish because it's a part of my heritage; but, the fact is, it wasn't until I started to make a business out of language learning that I finally took it seriously.

You don't have to start a business to learn languages, but you must know that you're building a real skill. If you haven't thought about the possible employment or promotion options, then now is the time to think about it.

Money isn't everything, but it could be a great motivator during the times where you think about quitting.

## **Misconceptions**

### **Only Children Can Learn Languages**

I blame the people who falsely report science studies, to get views, for this one.

Yes, children's brains may be more receptive to learning languages than adults, but that doesn't mean they are better learners.

As an adult, you're more aware of how languages work so you will have an easier time learning new concepts in a shorter period of time. The difference is, as a child, your only job was to learn a language.

People forget the sheer amount of time it took to become fluent in our first language. On average, it takes 8 years of constant 24/7 exposure, with study of the language, to become fluent.

The reason most people fail is not that children are better learners, it's because they never put in the hours necessary.

## **Dreaming in the language**

I've heard a weird rumor: If you dream in a language, you are fluent in the language. I was able to experience the falseness of this first hand.

Within a couple months of starting Japanese, I had a dream in Japanese. Does that mean I've become fluent? No. I only had a dream associated with Japanese.

The probable cause is due to the amount of time I spent studying.

When you sleep, your brain consolidates all the information that you have gathered throughout the day. If you do anything for long enough, you will have dreams about it.

I've even created my own dreams by controlling my thoughts before I went to sleep. Crazy, right? And disproves any logic behind this misconception.

Dreaming could be a good indicator you are doing something right; but, by no means, is it a definite sign you are fluent.

# **Thinking in the Language**

This is the opposite of dreaming. Dreams are filled with unconscious thoughts, while thinking takes effort.

Thinking in the language means you can produce thoughts and opinions in the target language without assistance from your native language.

For this reason, thinking shows a high level of fluency.

That said, you can aim for this, but you shouldn't expect it. The only way to get to this level is to have extensive exposure to the language; to the point where it becomes instinctive.

To think IN the language, you must not think ABOUT the language.

## **Native Speakers / Immersion**

I've seen many people over-value the importance of native speakers and immersion; as if having it, is the only way they would succeed in the language.

This is an excuse!

In reality, unless they are a native teacher (Native speaker who also teaches the language), native speakers are good for two things.

1. Practicing what you already know.

2. Answering individual questions you may have.

Most native speakers don't analyze the language as a learner would. They have instinctive knowledge of the language. Many of the questions you will have, the natives

# The Language Learner's Pocketbook

haven't thought about for years. They may not even know how to explain why. To them, it's just the way it is.

Teachers analyze the language and have to instruct the students on it; in this way, they are many times more valuable than a normal native. They give you structure.

The other part is immersion. Just because you are in the country, does not mean you're immersed.

If you work and live in your native language, friends and all, you can live in the country for years and never speak a lick of the foreign language.

You have to actively study the language. Passive study won't allow you to improve rapidly.

You learn the language to talk to natives and be immersed, not the other way around.

The amazing part of this digital age is that you can be more immersed in the comfort of your own home than people who live in the country.

There is no excuse for lack of immersion in today's day and age.

## **Learn One to Learn Another**

I have gotten asked, "Which language should I learn? [This language] or [that language]?"

Also, "Should I learn [this language] to help me learn [that language]?"

Deep down inside, they know which language they want to learn, but they let themselves get distracted.

ALWAYS go with the language you WANT to learn the most, even if it is more difficult.

Will learning one language help you to learn another? Yes, but first you have to learn that language and learning takes time.

Any time you spend learning one language, you take time away from the other. If you're not passionate about the language you will resent that wasted time. You might even quit before you start the language you're passionate about.

Always pick the language you have the most passion for, no matter the difficulty.

## **Two at the Same Time**

Generally, the people who ask about learning two languages at the same time, haven't even learned their first foreign language, yet. I love the enthusiasm, but: Slow down!

Many people barely spend the time to learn one language, let alone two.

If you learn two languages at once, you will be half as effective. You will either have to double the duration (Ex. From 3 to 6 years) or double the time per day.

To make any significant progress, you will need to study for an hour a day: Each! Which means you will need two hours every single day to get anywhere.

Even if you do have two hours, I would stick to one language at a time.

If you learn both from scratch this means you haven't built the skills to decipher each language; the information can mix. This mix could make the process longer for each language. Even if you reach the necessary hours, they won't be as effective.

Where would you rather be in two years?

> Fluent in one language and starting another or...

> Can barely get by in two languages.

You should only move onto another language once you have built the skills in the first language. This will prevent the time division and the mixing of information which will allow you to learn them, both, faster in the long run.

The Language Learner's Pocketbook

# **Watching Videos to Learn**

Watching videos can be helpful, but don't over value them.

The videos I'm talking about here are not instructional based videos meant to teach you the language. These are simply videos for entertainment, in the target language.

This goes back to the same reasons about native speakers except, here, you can't even ask questions!

Watching videos is comprehension practice. You practice what you already know, that's it. It can't be the only practice!

However, if you do the methods I talked about in Master Listening, watching videos can be highly beneficial.

The key difference is passive vs. active learning.

You will never learn if you only sit and watch. You must be active.

Mezasu.com

## **Free to Learn**

This is the one that annoys me the most because I was one of them and I know how much time it wastes.

I mentioned earlier, you have to expect to pay money if you are serious about learning languages.

The Big Reason: NOBODY is going to work for you for free.

You may get people who will trade free products for your attention, but these are likely to be free samples with the goal to get you to invest in the real service.

Free is code for: Not the full product.

If you don't get the full product, then you don't get the full benefits from learning.

AKA – You're wasting time.

---

End of Misconceptions

The Language Learner's Pocketbook

# **Tutors**

Tutors can be a great asset for the same reasons explained in Native Speakers / Immersion. They give you an outlet of instruction and immersion.

They will be able to spot and correct your mistakes while, also, giving you a template of what you should do next.

There are different types of tutors. Some are professional teachers; while others are more like talking partners. It's up to you to determine which one you need.

* Tip *

---

Your time with the tutor shouldn't be all of your study time. If you spend an hour with a tutor, you should aim for 10 hours of self-study. This is because they won't be there to get you through all the hours required to become fluent.

---

# **Burn Out**

The main reason you will suffer burn out is because you do the same exact routine day in and day out.

Even with the most efficient methods in the world, you're not a robot. The effectiveness degrades over time. The human mind grows bored and starts cutting corners. To keep this from happening, you must change what you do.

It could be a simple break from the norm to do something entertaining in the language.

I did this while learning Japanese. When my motivation was gone, but I still wanted to study, I picked up a manga (Japanese comic) and read for a few moments.

I don't try to analyze the language; I read. If I don't understand; I skip.

The goal is not to learn, but enjoy.

# The Language Learner's Pocketbook

By the time I'm done, I may re-spark my motivation to study; though, it's not always that easy.

This calls for serious change.

No matter what you've done or what you plan to do, you have to change the methods (Ex. textbook to video study).

This isn't a permanent change. You can do it for as little as a day. The goal is to break the routine so you can come back inspired.

Mezasu.com

# Conclusion

# **What Now?**

Now...you no longer have any reason to give an excuse. Now...the only one to blame is yourself.

JUST DO IT!!!

If you are truly dedicated and you follow everything in this book, you will be much better off than before. Whether you're able to get the results, or not, is up to you.

The single most important concept to take from this whole book is:

---

Those with the most active hours of study are the ones who get the most results. Nothing can replace active study time in the language!

---

As you start and/or progress in your journey, please stop by Mezasu.com.

It is built around social media where you can post, comment, and engage with other language learners. You can help people with your native language, as they can help you with theirs.

However, that is not what makes it special. We build tools integrated into the system which allow you to do more than interact with others. You are sure to find tools which use the methods talked about in this book.

I strive for only the best and you should, too.

I hope to see you at Mezasu.com!

---

If you would like to read more from me, you can visit:

CristianDavila.com

Here, I blog, not only about language learning, but self-improvement as a whole.

I wish you all the luck with your language learning...As if you'll need luck anymore ;)

www.ingramcontent.com/pod-product-compliance
Lightning Source LLC
Chambersburg PA
CBHW071209070526
44584CB00019B/2969